CHEROKEE

ᏣᎳᎩ

WORDS

ᎧᏁᏨᎢ ᎤᏪᏘ

With Pictures

BY

MARY ULMER CHILTOSKEY

THE STEPHENS PRESS

ASHEVILLE, NORTH CAROLINA 28803

2

Cherokee Alphabet.

D a	R e	T i	ꭳ o	O u	i v
S ga Ꮖ ka	F ge	Y gi	A go	J gu	E gv
Ꭵ ha	P he	Ꭷ hi	F ho	Γ hu	Ꮚ hv
W la	Ꮯ le	P li	G lo	M lu	Ꮃ lv
Ꮢ ma	Ꭰ me	H mi	Ꮍ mo	Y mu	
Θ na tᏂna Gnah	Λ ne	h ni	Z no	Ꮑ nu	O nv
T qua	Ꮄ que	P qui	V quo	Ꮖ quu	E quv
U sa Ꮃ s	4 se	b si	ꭲ so	Ᏽ su	R sv
L da W ta	S de Ꮅ te	Ꮧ di Ꮬ ti	V do	S du	Ᏸ dv
Ꮷ dla Ꮭ tla	L tle	C tli	Ꮏ tlo	Ꮺ tlu	P tlv
G tsa	V tse	Ir tsi	K tso	J tsu	Cᵂ tsv
G wa	Ꮃ we	Θ wi	Ꮼ wo	Ꮗ wu	6 wv
Ꮉ ya	B ye	Ꮛ yi	ꭶ yo	Gᵂ yu	B yv

Sounds represented by Vowels.

a, as a in father, or short as a in rival   o, as aw in law, or short as o in not.
e, as a in hate, or short as e in met   u, as oo in fool, or short as u in pull.
i, as i in pique, or short as i in pit   v, as u in but, nasalized.

Consonant Sounds

g nearly as in English, but approaching to k. d nearly as in English but approaching
to t. h k l m n q s t w y. as in English. Syllables beginning with g except Ꮣ have sometimes the
power of k. A. S. Ꮥ are sometimes sounded to, tu, tv, and Syllables written with tl except Ꮣ
sometimes vary to dl.

THE CHEROKEE ALPHABET

THIS LITTLE DICTIONARY is dedicated to the memory of Sequoyah and Will West Long, to the patience of Watty and Goingback and to my cats who kept me from working too long at one time

This is written for boys and girls of all ages who like Indians and especially for those who are interested in the Cherokee language. *Cherokee Words* may not teach you to use the language as well as the older Cherokee people, but with its help you will be able to say many of our English words in Cherokee. You may find your name in this book.

Many people helped make this book. The great Cherokee man Sequoyah by 1821 had invented a syllabary—something like an alphabet—so that his people could write their way of talking. His syllabary is in this book.

Years ago many Cherokee people could read, write and speak their language. Now only a few can. About 25 years ago Will West Long, who lived in Big Cove, began writing down words, phrases and sentences. He passed away before he made a book.

About two years ago these papers came to me. I tried unsuccessfully to complete his work. Maybe Mr. Long did not want me to carry on his work but to do it in my way. A page of his work is used to show you what a fine job he was doing.

I found in my own home the help needed: my brother-in-law, Watty Chiltoskie and my husband, Goingback Chiltoskey. Watty reads, writes and speaks his language. Goingback speaks it. We tried several lists, adding words suggested by interested people.

The "language gap" between English and Cherokee became very real as we worked. English has its own rules for spelling and pronunciation. Cherokee depends on sound. As a person hears a word, so he writes it. In cases of too much difference, we referred to the Bible translation. English words often have two correct ways of spelling, wild plants have several common names, so two Cherokee writers might write the same word with different characters. For pronunciation, see bottom of the Cherokee alphabet page which follows this.

For picture drawings we ran a contest in the Cherokee Indian Schools. Lib Lambert (now Mrs. John Langdale) was chosen as our illustrator.

Mary Gibbs was my standby for typing. George M. Stephens gave generously of his know-how. To both these friends I am grateful.

January 1972   MARY ULMER CHILTOSKEY

CHEROKEE WORDS

ᏣᎳᎩ ᏗᎧᏁᎢᏍᏗ
tsa la gi   di ka ne i s di

acorn ᎫᎴ
gu le

Amen ᎡᎺᏅ
e me nv

and ᎠᎴ
a le

anvil ᎠᏐᏗ ᏔᎷᎩᏍᎩ ᏅᎵᎩ
a so di ta lu gi s gi nv li gi

apple ᏍᎢᎦᏔ
sv ga ta

apron ᎠᏤᏎᏙ
a tse sa do

arrow ᏗᎦᏓᏟᏛ
di ga da tla dv

arrow-heads ᏗᎦᏓᏟᏛ ᏧᏍᎪ
di ga da tla dv tsu s go

ashes ᎪᏍᏚ
go s du

aunt ᎡᏠᎩ
e tlo gi

ax ᎦᎷᏯᏍᏗ
ga lu ya s di

baby ᎤᏍᏗᎦ
u s di ga

bad ᎤᏲᎢ
u yo i

bag ᏕᎦᎶᏗ
de ga lo di

ball ᎠᎳᏍᎦᏗ
a la s ga di

barrel ᏍᏙᏂ
sv do ni

basket ᏔᎷᏣ
ta lu tsa

bass (fish) ᎤᏃᎦ
u no ga

5

batter	DᏣᏒᏗ a su ge di	
beads	DᏋᏔ a de la	ᏗᏯᏦᏗ di ya tso di
bean	ᏚᏔ du ya	
bear	ᏱᎤ yo nv	
beaver	ᏙᏝ do yi	
bed	ᏩᏂᏏ ga ni si	
bee	ᏩᏚᏟᏏ wa du li si	
before	ᎢᎬᏱᏗᏝ i gv yi di tlv	
behind	ᎤᏂᏗᏝ o ni di tlv	
bell	ᎭᎸᏂ ha lv ni	
below	ᎡᎳᏗᏝ e la di tlv	
belt	ᎠᏓᏠᏍᏗ a da tlo s di	
bench	ᎦᏅᎯᏛ ga nv hi dv	ᎦᏍᎩᎶ ga s gi lo
beside	ᎤᏟᏗᏝ u li di tlv	
between	ᎠᏯᎵ a ye li	
Bible	ᎪᏪᎵ go we li	ᎤᎭᎨᏛ u ha ge dv
big	ᎡᏆ e qua	
bigger	ᎤᏔᏂᏗ u ta ni di	
bird	ᏥᏍᏆ tsi s qua	
birthday	ᎤᏕᏘᏱᏍᎬᎢ u de ti yi s gv i	

6

English	Cherokee
black	EΘⱢⲦ gv na ge i
blackbird	EΘⱢ ⱨ☉Ⲏ gv na ge tsi s qua
black-snake	Ꮪ♪Y ga le gi
blanket	♪☉ⲦᏫh tsu s qua u ni
blood	YE gi gv
blouse	DⱢB ᏚᏚⲦ ☉ꝰℰY a ge yv ga du i u lv wo gi
blue	ᏌAⱨⱢⲦ sa go ni ge i
bluebird	GꝬWⳑY tsa quo la da gi
boat	ⱨGᷱ tsi yu
bobcat	E𝓟 gv he
book	Aꝏⲅ go we li
box (n)	ᏚⱯᏌⲦ ga ne sa i
bow (hunting)	ᏚⲅGⱮ ga li tsa di
boy	DↄG a tsu tsa
boys	DⱨↄG a ni tsu tsa
branch (tree)	☉♪Ɱ ☉GhᏚꝯ u s di u wa ni ga lv
branch (stream)	☉♪ⰘⱢBⲦ u s di ge yv qua
brain	☉☌ⱨⳑ u nv tsi da
bread	ᏚᏚ ga du
bridge	DℛⱨΗ a sv tsi

7

broad ax ᎤᏛᎾ ᎦᎷᏯᏍᏗ
u dv na ga lu ya s di

brothers ᎠᎾᏓᏅᏟ
a na da nv tli

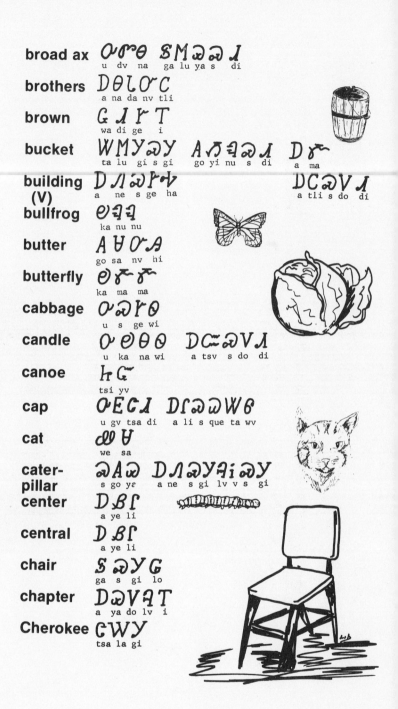

brown ᏩᏗᎨᎢ
wa di ge i

bucket ᏔᎷᎩᏍᎩ ᎪᏱᏄᏍᏗ ᎠᎹ
ta lu gi s gi go yi nu s di a ma

building (V) ᎠᏁᏍᎨᎭ ᎠᏟᏍᏙᏗ
a ne s ge ha a tli s do di

bullfrog ᎧᏄᏄ
ka nu nu

butter ᎪᏌᏅᎯ
go sa nv hi

butterfly ᎧᎹᎹ
ka ma ma

cabbage ᎤᏍᎨᏫ
u s ge wi

candle ᎤᎧᎾᏫ ᎠᏨᏍᏙᏗ
u ka na wi a tsv s do di

canoe ᏥᏴ
tsi yv

cap ᎤᎬᏣᏗ ᎠᎵᏍᏇᏔᏮ
u gv tsa di a li s que ta wv

cat ᏪᏌ
we sa

cater-pillar ᏍᎪᏯ ᎠᏁᏍᎩᎸᎥᏍᎩ
s go ya a ne s gi lv v s gi

center ᎠᏰᎵ
a ye li

central ᎠᏰᎵ
a ye li

chair ᎦᏍᎩᎶ
ga s gi lo

chapter ᎠᏯᏙᎸᎢ
a ya do lv i

Cherokee ᏣᎳᎩ
tsa la gi

English	Cherokee	Phonetic
Cherokee (place)	ᏣᎳᎩᏱ	tsa la gi yi
cherry	ᏔᏯ	ta ya
chestnut	ᏘᎵ	ti li
chicken	ᏣᏔᎦ	tsa ta ga
child	ᎠᏲᏟ	a yo tli
children	ᏗᏂᏲᏟ	di ni yo tli
chimney	ᎠᏚᏦᏩᎳᎬᎢ	a hu tsa wa la gv i
chipmunk	ᎩᏳᎦ	gi yu ga
Christmas	ᎤᎾᏕᏘᏱᏍᎬᎢ	u na de ti yi s gv i
cloth	ᎠᎾᏬ	a na wo
cloud	ᎤᎶᎩᎸ	u lo gi lv
coat	ᎦᏌᎴᎾ	ga sa le na
coffee	ᎪᏪ	go we
cold	ᎤᏴᏝ	u yv tla
colt	ᎠᎩᎾ ᏠᏈᎵ	a gi na so qui li
container	ᎠᏟᏍᏙᏗ	a tli s do di
cook (n)	ᎠᏓᏍᏓᏴᎲᏍᎩ	a da s da yv hv s gi
cook (v)	ᎠᏓᏍᏓᏴᎲ	a da s da yv hv
copperhead	ᏬᏗᎨ ᎠᏍᎪᎵ	wo di ge a s go li
corn	ᏎᎷ	se lu

9

corner	OᎶᏏᏴᎢ
	u nv si yv i
cove	OᏏᏞᏗᏴᎢ
	u ge da li yv i
cow	ᏀᏍ
	wa ga
crawfish	ᎭᎦᏲᎾ
	tsi s dv na
creek	ᎯᏫᏡᎫ
	ni la dv yi
cricket	ᏉᏉᏚ
	ta la du
crow	ᎪᎬ
	go gv
cucumber	ᏎᏎᎹ
	ga ga ma
cup	ᏎᏄᎯᎶᏗ
	ga nu hi lo di
daughter	ᎠᏇᎭ ᎠᏥᎤᏣ
	a que tsi a ge yu tsa
day	ᎢᏍ
	i ga
daylight	OᎩᎭᎿ
	u gi tsi ha
deep	ᎭᏫᏂ
	ha wi ni
deer	ᎠᏫ
	a wi
devil	ᎠᏍᎩᎾ
	a s gi na
dime	ᏍᎪ ᎢᏯᏓᏅᏖᏗ
	s go i ya da nv te di
dirt	ᎦᏓ
	ga da
doctor	ᏗᏓᏅᏫᏍᎩ
	di da nv wi s gi
dog	ᎩᎵ
	gi li
dogwood	ᎧᏅᏏᏔ
	ka nv si ta

face	$O \ominus \cap T$ u ka dv i	
fast	$SG \exists W$ ga lo nu la	
fat	$O \cap K \mathcal{A} \cap$ u li tso hi dv	
father	RVL e do da	
feather	$O y l J$ u gi da li	
field	$K \mathcal{V} b$ tso ge si	
fireplace	$A \cap \mathcal{A}$ $D \Gamma C e W \cap T$ go dv di a hu tsa wo la dv i	
first	$DE \mathcal{I} \mathcal{A}$ a gv yi yi	
fish	DCA a tsa di	
fishing	$D \mathcal{C} i \mathcal{D} y$ a su v s gi	
flour	$O \mathcal{C} \mathcal{P} \mathcal{D} L$ u tsa le s da	
flower	$\Gamma h \mathcal{A} \mathcal{P}$ hu tsi lv ha	
flowing	RET e gv i	
fly (n)	$\cap S$ dv ga	
fog (far)	$JE \mathcal{P} \cap$ tsu gv ha dv	
forest	$DV \mathcal{A}$ a do hi	
forever	$\mathcal{V} 4 \mathcal{D} \mathcal{J}$ ge se s ti	
fox	JW tsu la	
friend	$\mathcal{D} y \ominus \Gamma T$ o gi na li i	
friends	$KS \Gamma T$ tso ga li i	

door ᎦᎶᎯᏍᏗ
ga lo hi s di

doorway ᎦᎶᎯᏍᏗᏱ
ga lo hi s di yi

dough (corn) ᎠᏑᎨᏓ ᏎᎷ
a su ge da se lu

dough flour) ᎠᏑᎨᏓ ᎤᎶᎴᏍᏓ
a su ge da u lo le s da

dove ᎫᎴ ᏗᏍᎪᏂᎯ
gu le di s go ni hi

down ᎡᎳᏗ
e la di

dress ᎠᏌᏃ
a sa no

duck ᎦᏩᏅ
ga wa nv

eagle ᎤᏬᎭᎵ
u wo ha li

ear ᎦᎴ
ga le

earth ᎡᎶᎯᏃ
e lo hi no

east ᎧᎸᎬᎢ
ka lv gv i

eat ᎯᎦ
hi ga

eel ᏛᏕᎩ
dv de gi

egg ᎤᏪᏥ
u we tsi

eggs ᎫᏪᏥ
gu we tsi

elephant ᎧᎹᎹ
ka ma ma

enemy ᏦᏥᏓᎾᏩ
tso tsi da na wa

eye ᎠᎦᏙᎵ
a ga do li

eyes ᏗᎦᏙᎵ
di ga do li

frog	ᎦᏌᏆ wa lo si	
frost	ᎤᏯᏛᎭ u ya dv ha	
gap (mtn)	ᎤᏴᎳᏛᏛᎢ u yv la dv dv i	
garden	ᎠᏫᏒᏗᏱ a wi sv di yi	
girl	ᎠᎨᏳᏣ a ge yu tsa	
glass	ᎤᏁᏍᏓᎳ u ne s da la	
gloves	ᏗᎵᏰᏑᎶ di li ye su lo	
goat	ᏧᏍᏆᏁᎩᏛ tsu s qua ne gi dv	
God	ᎡᏙᏓ e do da	
gold	ᏓᎶᏂᎨᎢ da lo ni ge i	
goose	ᏎᏎ sa sa	
grapes	ᏆᎷᏏ qua lu si	
grass	ᎦᏄᎸᎯ ga nu lv hi	
grass- hopper	ᏙᎳᏧᎦ do la tsu ga	
gravy	ᎤᎦᎹ u ga ma	
gritter	ᎠᏑᎪᏍᏗ ᏎᎷ ᏧᏩᏂᎨᎢ a su gos di se lu tsu wa ni ge i	
green	ᎠᏤᎯ a tse hi	
ground- hog	ᎣᎦᎾ o ga na	
group	ᎤᏓᏟᎩ u da tli gi	
groups	ᎤᎾᏓᏟᎩ u na da tli gi	

13

guinea (fowl) ᎫᏇ ᏗᎦᎾᏌᎢ — gu que di ga na sa i

hammer ᎬᏂ ᎵᏓᏍᏓ — gv ni li da s da

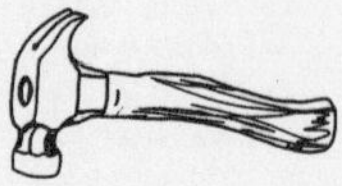

hand ᎤᏩᏱ — u wa yi

handsaw ᎤᏍᏗᎠ ᎦᎾᏙᎩ — u s di a ga na do gi

hat ᎠᎵᏍᏇᏔᏬᎩ — a li s que ta wo gi

hay ᎧᏁᏍᎦ — ka ne s ga

hazelnut ᎠᏳᎩᏛ — a yu gi dv

head ᎠᏍᎪᎵ — a s go li

hear ᎦᏛᎩᎠ — ga dv gi a

heat ᎤᏗᎴᎦ — u di le ga

heaven ᎦᎸᎳᏗ — ga lv la di

hello ᏏᏳ — si yu

heron ᎧᎾᏍᎪᏩ — k na s go wa

highway ᎡᏆ ᏅᏃᎯ — e qua nv no hi

hoe ᎦᎶᎪᏗ — ga lo go di

hog ᏏᏆ — si qua

holly ᎤᏍᏓᏍᏗ — u s da s di

home ᎠᏇᏅᏒᎢ — a que nv sv i

hominy ᎦᏃᎮᏅ — ga no he nv

horse ᏐᏈᎵ — so qui li

hot	ᎤᏗᎴᎦ	u di le ga
house	ᎠᏓᏁᎸ	a da ne lv
humming-bird	ᎬᎴᎷ	wa le lu
hurry	ᎤᏟᏍᏓ	u tli s da
husband	ᎤᏰᎯ	u ye hi
ice	ᎤᏁᏓᎳ	u ne s da la
icicle	ᎤᏁᏓᎳ ᎤᏁᏌᏛᎢ	u ne s da la u ne sa dv i
inch	ᎡᏯᏏᏔᏛᎯ	e ya si ta dv hi
Indian	ᏴᏫᏯᎯ	yv wi ya hi
Indians	ᎠᏂ ᏴᏫᏯᎯ	a ni yv wi ya hi
inside	ᎭᏫᏂ	ha wi ni
island	ᎠᎹᏰᎵ	a ma ye li
itch	ᎤᏂᏥᎳ	u ni tsi la
Jehovah	ᏱᎰᎳ	yi ho wa
Jesus	ᏥᏌ	tsi sa
jug	ᎦᏓᎫᎫ	ga da gu gu
jump	ᎭᏓᎾᏫᏛ	ha da na wi dv
kettle	ᎧᏫ ᎠᏙᏗ ᏧᎳᏍᎩ	ka wi a do di tsu la s gi
key	ᎠᏍᏕᎢᏍᏗ	a s de i s di
kill	ᏥᎷᎦ	tsi lu ga

knife	ᏴᏪᏲᏗ	ye la s di
lake	ᎥᏓᏟ	v da li
lamp	ᎠᏨᏲᏗ ᎪᎢ	a tsv s di go i
learn	ᎦᏙᎴᏆ	ga do le qua
leg	ᎦᎦᏃᎢ	ga ga lo i
legs	ᏗᎦᎦᏃᎢ	di ga ga lo i
light	ᎤᎸᏌᏓ ᎠᏨᏍᏛᎢ	u lv sa da a tsa s dv i
like (looks)	ᏹᏂᏠᏯ	gi ni tlo yi
lion	ᏛᏓᏥ	tlv da tsi
lives (v)	ᎡᎭ	e ha
log	ᏧᎸᏓᎨᏫ	tsu lv da ge wi
long	ᎦᏅᎯᏛ	ga nv hi dv
love	ᏥᎸᏉᏗ or ᏥᎨᏳᎢ	tsi lv quo di tsi ge yu i
man	ᎠᏍᎦᏯ	a s ga ya
mask	ᎠᎬᏚᏉ	a gv du lo
match (n)	ᎠᏧᏲᏗ	a tsu s di
mattress	ᎠᏤᏲᏙ	a tse s do
meat	ᎭᏫᏯ	ha wi ya
medicine	ᏅᏩᏘ	nv wa ti
men	ᎠᏂᏍᎦᏯ	a ni s ga ya

16

metal	ᏔᎷᎩᏍᎩ	ta lu gi s gi
milk	ᎤᏅᏗ	u nv di
minister	ᎠᎳᏥᏙᎶᏍᎩ	a la tsi do lo s gi
minnow	ᎤᏍᏗ ᎠᏣᏗ	u s di a tsa di
minnows	ᏧᎾᏍᏗ ᎠᏣᏗ	tsu na s di a tsa di
moccasin (shoe)	ᎤᏧᏬᏗ	u tsu wo di
mole	ᏘᏁᏆ	ti ne qua
money	ᎠᏕᎳ	a de la
month	ᎢᏯᏅᏓ	i ya nv da
moon	ᎤᏙ ᏒᏃᎢ Ꭿ	u do sv no e hi
mosquito	ᏙᏌ ᎤᏛᎾ	do sa u dv na
mother	ᎡᏥ	e tsi
mountain	ᎤᏅᏓᏢᎢ	u nv da tlv i
mountains	ᏚᏅᏓᏢᎢ	du nv da tlv i
mouse (shrew)	ᏔᎳᏍᎨᏫ	ta la s ge wi
mouth	ᎠᎰᎵ	a ho li
mulberry	ᎫᏩ	gu wa
(brown) mushroom (edible)	ᎤᎶᏇ	u lo que
(brown) mushrooms (edible)	ᎤᏂᎶᏇ	u ni lo que
muskrat	ᏌᎳᏈᏍᎩ	sa la qui s gi

17

nail	BY yv gi	
needle	SBOƏVᴧ BY ga ye wi s do di yv gi	
Negro	EᏇᏒT gv na ge i	
nephew	iƳθθ v gi wi na	
new	Dⱱᴧ a tse hi	
news-paper	ᴧSSBWOᴧ AꙄꙂ di ga le yv ta nv hi go we li	
nickel (coin)	AꙂƳ TꙂlOƼᴧ hi s gi i ya da nv te di	
night	RZᴦ sv no yi	
no	ᏝZ tla no	
none	ƏhƳᝋ ka ni gi dv	
north	ᏠBPT tsu yv tlv i	
nose	SB+ꙅ ga yv so li	
now	Zⱱ no quo	
old	DꙄBꙅ a ga yv li	
onion	RƳ sv gi	
open	DꙂSTᝋ a s du i dv	
outside	VBᴧ do ye hi	
overalls	Oⱱᴧᴧ DᏟG u tse sa di a su lo	
overcoat	Oᝑθ SᏬꙄθ u dv na ga sa le na	
owl	OᏠᏠ u gu gu	

18

paid	DJBᎲ		
	a gu yo dv		
paint (n)	DᏏᎾᎾᎿ		
	a si wi s ti		
pair	ᏌᏦᏝ		
	tsu tso da li		
panther	ᏢᏝᎭ		
	tlv da tsi		
paper	AᏪᏝ		
	go we li		
part-ridge	ᏌᏪ		
	gu que		
passage-way	ᏎᎮᏄᏛᎢ		
	ga ne nu tlv i		
path	ᎤᏍᏗ	ᏅᏃᎯ	ᎤᎶᎯᏍᏗ
	u s di	nv no hi	u lo hi s di
pay	DJBᏗ		
	a gu yv di		
peace	ᎥᎯᏫ		
	do hi vi		
peach	ᏆᎾᎥ		
	qua nv		
peacock	ᎬᎾ ᏌᏔᏆᏙᏟ		
	gv na tau qua to tli		
pear	ᏎᏗ ᎢᏳᏍᏗ ᏒᎦᏔ		
	se di i yu s di sv ga ta		
pencil	ᎵᎪᏪᎶᏗ		
	li go we lo di		
persimmon	ᏌᎵ		
	sa li		
pheasant	ᎲᏗᏍᏗ		
	dv di s di		
pillow	DJᎦᎥ		
	a gu s do		
pine	ᏃᏥ		
	no tsi		
pineapple	ᏃᏥ ᏔᏘᏎᏗ ᏒᎦᏔ		
	no tsi i yu s di sv ga ta		
pink	ᎤᏍᎪᎸ ᎩᎦᎮᎢ		
	u s go lv gi ga ge i		

pitcher	OꙨ4Ꙇ	u we se di
place	ᏂᎾᎯ	ha na ni
plate	ᎦᏓᏙ	te li do
plates	ᏗᎦᏓᏙ	di te li do
play (v)	ᏔᏁᎶᎲᏍᎦ	da ne lo hv s ga
plow	ᎦᏓᎷᎪᏗ	ga da lu go di
plum	ᏆᏄᎾᏍᏗ	qua nu na s di
poplar	ᏥᏳ	tsi yu
pony	ᎤᏍᏗᎠ ᏐᏈᎵ	u s di a so qui li
potato	ᏄᎾ	nu nv
preacher	ᎠᎳᏥᏙᎰᏍᎩ	a la tsi do ho s gi
pumpkin	ᎢᏯ	i ya
quail	ᏆᏇ	qu que
Qualla	ᏆᎸᏱ	qua lv yi
quiet	ᎡᎶᏪᎯ	e lo we hi
quilt	ᏎᎦᎵ	ye ga li
quilts	ᏗᏎᎦᎵ	di ye ga li
quit	ᏥᏲᎯᏍᏓ	tsi yo hi s da
rabbit	ᏥᏍᏚ	tsi s du
raccoon	ᎬᎵ	gv li

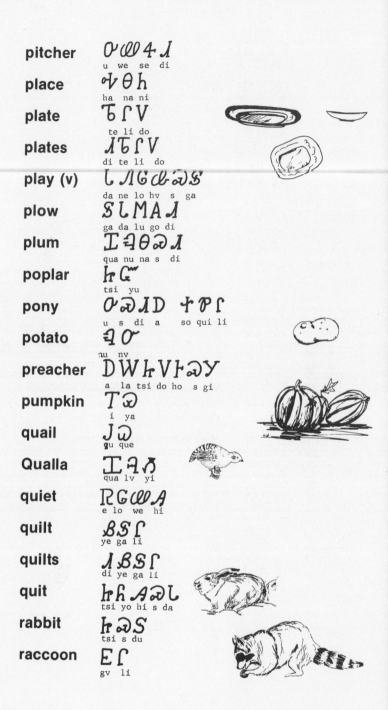

20

rain-ing	DᏕᏆᏕ	a ga s ga
rain-bow	ᎣᏅᏊᏩᏞ	u nv quo la da
rat	ᏥᏕᏎᏥ	tsi s de tsi
rattle	ᏚᎾᏤᏗ	ga na tse di
rattle-snake	ᎤᏦᎾᏘ	u tso na ti
raven	ᎪᎳᏅ	go la nv
read (pres)	ᎯᎪᎵᏯ	hi go li ya
red	ᎩᎦᎨᎢ	gi ga ge i
red-bird	ᏙᏧᏩ	do tsu wa
return	ᎱᎷᏣ	hu lu tsa
rice	ᎪᏃᎮᏅ	go no he nv
river	ᎡᏉᏂ ᎨᏴᎢ	e quo ni ge yv i
ring (n)	ᎠᎵᏤᏑᏍᏔᏬ	a li ye su s ta wo
robin	ᏥᏕᏉᏉ	tsi s quo quo
rock	ᏅᏯ	nv ya
rough (in play)	ᎤᏓᏣᏛᏗ	u da tsa dv di
run	ᏘᏍᏆᎸᏓ	ti s qua lv da
salt	ᎠᎹ	a ma
sassafras	ᎧᎾᏍᏓᏥ	ka na s da tsi
saw (n)	ᎦᎾᏙᏱ	ga na do yi

21

school	$\mathcal{V}\mathcal{V}\mathcal{S}\mathcal{I}\mathcal{Q}\mathcal{A}$	di do le qua s di
see	$\mathcal{H}A\mathcal{G}\mathcal{J}\mathcal{V}$	tsi go wa ti ha
sew	$\mathcal{S}\mathcal{B}\Theta\mathcal{Q}\mathcal{A}$	ga ye wi s di
sheep	$\mathcal{O}\mathcal{Z}\mathcal{S}\Theta$	u no de na
sheet	$\mathcal{O}\mathcal{W}\mathcal{Z}\mathcal{A}$	u ta no hi
shell	$\mathcal{O}\mathcal{D}\mathcal{Q}\mathcal{S}$	u ya s ga
shirt	$\mathcal{D}\mathcal{Q}\mathcal{S}\mathcal{B}$ $\mathcal{O}\mathcal{Q}\mathcal{Q}\mathcal{A}$	a s ga yv u nu wo hi
shoe	$\mathcal{D}\mathcal{W}\mathcal{Q}\mathcal{G}$	a la su lo
shoes	$\mathcal{I}\mathcal{W}\mathcal{Q}\mathcal{G}$	di la su lo
short	$\mathcal{Q}\mathcal{I}\mathcal{W}\mathcal{A}$	s qua la hi
sick	$\mathcal{O}\mathcal{P}\mathcal{S}$	u tlv ga
silver	$\mathcal{D}\mathcal{S}\mathcal{A}$	a de lv
sister	$\mathcal{T}\mathcal{Y}\mathcal{V}$	i gi do
skirt	$\mathcal{D}\mathcal{V}\mathcal{Z}$	a sa no
sky	$\mathcal{S}\mathcal{A}\mathcal{G}\mathcal{T}$	ga lv lo i
sleep	$\mathcal{S}\mathcal{C}\mathcal{V}$	ga tli ha
snail	$\mathcal{R}\mathcal{W}\mathcal{I}$	e la qua
snake	$\mathcal{T}\Theta\mathcal{O}$	i na dv
snow	$\mathcal{O}\mathcal{H}$	u nu tsi
snow-bird	$\mathcal{S}\mathcal{J}$	du di

sock (n)	ᎠᎵᎰ	a li ho
socks	ᏗᎵᎰ	di li ho
Soco	ᏌᏉ	sa quo
soldiers	ᎠᏂᏲᏫᏍᎩ	a ni yo wi s gi
someone	ᎩᎶ ᏌᏉᎯ	gi lo sa quo hi
son (of another)	ᎤᏪᏥᏛᎯ	u we tsi dv hi
soup	ᎤᎦᎹ	u ga ma
south	ᏧᎦᎾᏮᎢ	tsu ga na wv i
speckled	ᎤᏅᏣᏛ	u nv tsa dv
spice-wood	ᏃᏓᏥ	no da tsi
spoon	ᏗᏙᏗ	di do di
spring (of water)	ᎦᏄᎪᎬ ᎠᎹ	ga nu go gv a ma
squirrel	ᏌᎶᎵ	sa lo li
star	ᏃᏢᏏ	no tlv si
stool	ᎠᎵᏍᏛᏧᏍᏗ ᎦᏍᎩᎶ	a li s dv tsu s di ga s gi lo
stove	ᎠᏓᏍᏓᏗ ᎦᎧᎲᎢ	a da s da di ga ka hv i
straw-berry	ᎠᏅ	a nv
sugar	ᎦᎵᏎᏥ	ga li se tsi
sun	ᎢᎦ ᎡᎯ ᏅᏙ	i ga e hi nv do
sunshine	ᎠᎦᎵᎭ	a ga li ha

sweet	ᎤᏓᎾᏬᏛ	
	u ga na s dv	
table	ᏗᎵᏍᏓᏴᏗ ᎦᏍᎩᎶ	
	a li s da yv di ga s gi lo	
tail	ᎦᏙᎦ	
	ga do ga	
tails	ᏗᎦᏙᎦ	
	di ga do ga	
tales	ᎧᏃᎮᎸᎥᏍᎩ	
	ka no he lv v s gi	
talk	ᎯᏬᏂᎯ	
	hi wo ni hi	
tall	ᎦᎸᎳᏗ ᎢᎦᏗ	
	ga lv la di i ga di	
teacher	ᏗᏕᏲᎰᏍᎩ	
	di de yo ho s gi	
tears (rips)	ᎯᏦᎦᎸ	
	hi tsa ga lv	
tears (cry)	ᏧᎦᏌᏬᏛ	
	tsu ga sa wo dv	
teeth	ᏗᎦᏴᎦ	
	di ga yv ga	
tepee (cloth)	ᎠᎾᏬ ᎠᏓᏁᎥ	
	a na wo a da ne iv	
tepee (skin)	ᎦᏁᎦ ᎠᏓᏁᎥ	
	ga ne ga a da ne lv	
thick	ᎤᎭᎨᏛ	
	u ha ge dv	
thistle	ᏥᏥ	
	tsi tsi	
tobacco	ᏦᎸ	
	tso lv	
today	ᎪᎯ ᎢᎦ	
	go hi i ga	
toma-hawk	ᎦᎷᏯᏍᏗ	
	ga lu ya s di	
tomato	ᎤᎾᎫᏂᏍᏗ	
	u na gu hi s di	
tomatoes	ᎤᏂᎾᎫᏂᏍᏗ	
	u ni na gu hi s di	

24

to-morrow	ᏩᎾᎴᎢ su na le i	
tonight	ᎪᎯ Ꮙ ᏒᎯ go hi u sv hi	
tooth	ᎧᏳᎦ ka yu ga	
trail	ᎤᏍᏗ us di	ᏅᏃᎯ nv no hi
tree	ᏘᎷᎬᎢ tlu gv i	
trou-sers	ᎠᏧ Ꮅ a su lo	
turkey	ᎬᎾ gv na	
turnip	ᏓᏆᏌᏅ da qua sa nv	
twin	ᏗᎦᏢᏩ di ga tla wa	
twins	ᏗᏂᏢᏩ di ni tla wa	
uncle	ᎡᏚᏥ e du tsi	
under	ᎠᏫᏂᏌ a wi ni tsa	
up	ᎦᎸᎳᏗ ga lv la di	
valley	ᎨᏓᎵᏴᎢ ge da li yv i	
vein	ᎤᎶᎢᏍᏗ u lo i s di	ᎩᎬ gi gv
walnut	ᏎᏗ se di	
war	ᏓᎾᏩ da na wa	
warm	ᎤᎦᎾᏩ u ga na wa	
water	ᎠᎹ a ma	
weasel	ᏥᏍᎦᏥ tsi s ga tsi	ᏓᎶᏂ da lo ni

weeds	ᏕᎾᎵᎯ
	ga nu lv hi
welcome	ᏡᎵᎡᏟᎩ
	ga li e li gi
west	ᎤᏕᎵᎬᎢ
	wu de li gv i
wheat	ᎤᏣᎴᏍᏗ
	u tsa le s di
white	ᎤᏁᎦ
	u ne ga
wife	ᎠᏥᏰᎯ
	a tsi ye hi
wild	ᎨᏯᏔᎯ
	ge ya ta hi
wild-cat	ᎬᎮ
	gv he
wind	ᎤᏃᎴ
	u no le
window	ᏦᎳᏂ
	tso la ni
witch	ᏍᎩᎵ
	s gi li
wolf	ᏩᏯ
	wa ya
woman	ᎠᎨᏳ
	a ge yv
wood	ᎠᏓ
	a da
word	ᎧᏁᎢᏍᏗ
	ka ne i s di
words	ᏗᎧᏁᎢᏍᏗ
	di ka ne i s di
wren	ᏥᏥ
	tsi tsi
write	ᎰᏪᎸᎦ
	ho we lv ga
yellow	ᏓᎶᏂᎨᎢ
	da lo ni ge i
yes	ᎥᎥ
	v v

yester- Ꮎ ᏢᎯ
day u tlv hi
young ᎠᏞᎯ
a da hi

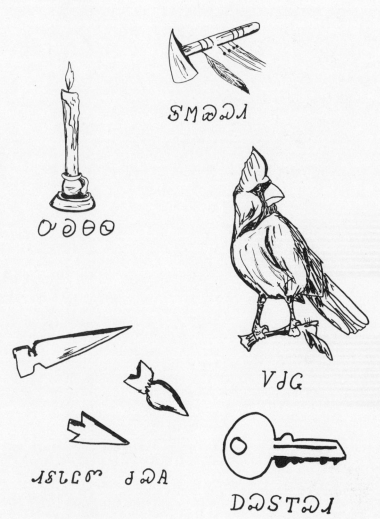

ᏚᎷᏇᎮᎠᎯ

Ꮎ ᎧᎯᎯ

ᏆᎫᎬ

ᏘᏕᎷᏟᏫ ᎫᏇᎯ

ᎠᏕᏚᏟᎠᎯ

27

SEQ

I N TWELVE Y
no schooling
others gave h
guage so simpl
read in a short t
Using the wl
ten words, whic
tures", Sequoya
and divided the
For each sour
English or Ger
86 characters ir
lable word need
This book is
nearly 500 wor
ber of names ar
it can show "ho

FROM THE CHARLES BIRD KING PORTRAIT

SEQUOYAH grew up in sight of the Smokies at Tuskegee village near old
Fort Loudoun. After he gained renown as a language scholar he sat for this
portrait in Washington about 1828. His statue is in the Capitol.

PHOTO BY JUANITA WILSON

MARY ULMER CHILTOSKEY,
librarian at Cherokee, wrote it.

PHOTO BY JUANITA WILSON

GOINGBACK CHILTOSKEY,
her husband, helped design it.

CAME TO BE

A H

Cherokee with
ttle help from
e a written lan-
nany learned to

's idea of writ-
led "talking pic-
Cherokee words
sounds.

ose a letter from
ges he found—
Thus a three-syl-
three characters.
nary translating
an equal num-
ses. With study
it in Cherokee".

PHOTO BY J. HOWARD BERRY

WILL WEST LONG lived in Big Cove in the Smokies near Cherokee, North Carolina. This picture made about 1940 shows him writing Sequoyah's language. Scholars came to learn from him about Cherokee lore.

PHOTO BY JUANITA WILSON

WATTY CHILTOSKIE, brother-in-law, did the language parts.

PHOTO BY CODY LAMBERT

LIB LAMBERT LANGDALE, Cherokee School, drew pictures.

Phrases, etc.

all right ꮂꭺ
ha wa

anothers grandmother ꭱꮟꮅ
e li si

bad looking ꮼꭽꭲ ꮈꭼꮓꮅꭹ
u ho i   di ka no di yi

barber shop ꮅꮣꮝꮩꮧꭹ
di da s   do di yi

bean bread ꮡꮹ ꭶꮪ
du ya   ga du

big spoon ꭱꮫ ꮧꮩꮧ
e qua   di do di

black racer (snake) ꭰꮩꭹꮿꭰꭹ ꭲꮎꮣꮡ
a do gi ya a gi   i na dv

black skunk ꮧꮬ
di la

blue jay ꮳꮿꭶ
tsa yo ga

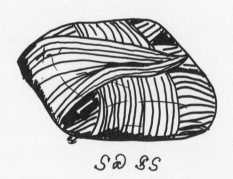

ꭶꮪ

bow & arrow ᏣᎵᏦᏗ ᎠᎴ ᏗᎦᏓᏘᏴ
ga li tsa di   a le   di ga da tla dv

butterbean game ᏚᏯ ᏗᏆᎾᏲᏍᏗ
du ya   di qua na yo s di

castiron pot ᏧᎳᏍᎩ
tsu la s gi

Cherokee Nation ᏣᎳᎩᏱ ᎠᏰᎵ
tsa la gi yi   a ye li

Cherokee Township ᏣᎳᎩᏱ ᏕᎦᏚᏩᏗᏒᎢ
tsa la gi yi   de ga du wa di sv i

Big Cove (Raven Place) ᎪᎳᏅᏱ
go la nv yi

Birdtown ᏥᏍᏉᎯ
tsi s quo hi

Paint-town ᏂᏬᏗᎯ
ni wo di hi

Snowbird ᏥᏱᎯ
tsi yi hi

Wolf-town ᏩᏲᎯ
wa yo hi

Yellow Hill ᎡᎳᏬᏗᎯ
e la wo di hi

chestnut bread ᏘᎵ ᎦᏚ
ti li   ga du

chestnut tree ᏘᎵ ᏟᎬᎢ
ti li   tlu gv i

chicken hawk ᏓᏬᏗ
ta wo di

coffee pot ᎧᏫ ᎠᏙᏗ ᏧᎳᏍᎩ
ka wi   a do di   tsu la s gi

Come in! ᎩᏴᎭ
gi yv ha

cooking pot ᏧᎳᏍᎩ
tsu la s gi

cooking stove ᎠᏓᏍᏓᏯᏗ ᎦᎧᎲᎢ
a da s da ya di   ga ka hv i

conch shell ᎡᎵᏆ ᎠᎹ ᎡᏆᎯᎡᎯ
e le qua   a ma   e qua hi e hi

corn beater ᎧᏃᎾ
ka no na

31

corn bread 4M ꮪꮪ
se lu ga du

corn dough DꮯꝠꮝ 4M
a su ge da se lu

Council Fire woods ꭾhꮃꭾꭹ Dꮅ ꮎꮓꮩꮏ
di ni la wi gi a da u no do ti

hickory Gꭺꭲ
wa ne i

oak Dꮩꮹꭿ
a da ya hi

maple CꮝGꭹ
tsv wa gi

locust ꭷGꮼꭹꭵ
ka lo que gi di

birch Dꮵꮢꭹ
a ti sv gi

beech ꮫꭱ
gu sv

ash ꮵꮪꮒꮕ
tsu ga no nv

Cullowhee ꭷꮃꮻꭹ
ka la wi yi

Days ꮪꮠꮣꭲꮢ
du do da qui sv

Monday ꮣꮪꮄꮕꭿ
do da quo nv hi

Tuesday ꮤꮅꮑꭲꭶ
ta li ne i ga

Wednesday ꮵꮟꮑꭲꭶ
tso i ne i ga

Thursday ꭴꭹꮑꭲꭶ
u gi ne i ga

Friday ꮵꮎꭹꮆꮝꮧ
tsu nagi lo s ti

Saturday ꮣꮣꭹꮥꮎ
do da qui de na

Sunday ꮣꮣꮖꮝꭶꭲ
do da qua s gv i

digging in several places ꮤꮝꭺꮃ
ta s go la

do you know? $\mathcal{A}\mathcal{S}\mathsf{W}\mathsf{o}\mathsf{J}$
hi ga ta ka tsu

do you want bread? $\mathsf{C}\mathsf{S}\mathsf{\Gamma}\mathsf{o}\mathsf{J}$ $\mathcal{S}\mathcal{S}$
tsa du li ha tsu   ga du

dough tray $\mathsf{D}\mathcal{C}\mathsf{\Gamma}\mathsf{V}\mathcal{A}$
a su ge do di

down the hill $\mathsf{\Gamma}\mathsf{L}\mathsf{\Gamma}$
ge da li

elm tree $\mathsf{L}\;\mathsf{G}\mathsf{h}\mathsf{W}$ $\mathcal{P}\mathsf{E}\mathsf{T}$
da wa tsi la   tlu gv i

empty vessel $\mathsf{D}\mathsf{h}\mathsf{\partial}\mathsf{V}\mathcal{A}$
a tsi s do di

falling flowers $\mathsf{h}\mathsf{W}\mathsf{V}\mathcal{J}\mathsf{\partial}\mathsf{Y}$
tsi la do o s gi

fat meat $\mathcal{O}\mathsf{\Gamma}\mathsf{C}\mathcal{A}\mathsf{T}$ $\mathsf{D}\mathsf{O}\mathsf{\partial}$
u li tsa hi dv   a we ya

flour corn $4\mathsf{M}$ $\mathsf{\partial}\mathcal{A}$
se lu   ya hi

flour dough $\mathsf{D}\mathcal{C}\mathsf{\Gamma}\mathsf{L}$ $\mathcal{O}\mathsf{G}\mathsf{P}\mathsf{\partial}\mathsf{L}$
a su ge da   u lo le s da

flying squirrel $\mathcal{S}\;\mathsf{G}$
de wa

frying pan $\mathsf{D}\mathsf{v}\mathsf{O}\mathsf{\partial}$ $\mathsf{E}\mathsf{O}\mathsf{G}\mathsf{V}\mathcal{A}$
a ha wi ya   gv na wa do di

Get into the water $\mathsf{v}\mathsf{W}\mathsf{W}\mathsf{S}\mathcal{S}$ $\mathsf{D}\mathsf{r}\mathcal{J}$
ha la ta du ga   a ma yi

glass bottle $\mathsf{J}\mathsf{J}$
gu gu

Go out! $\mathsf{V}\mathcal{J}$
do yi

go to work $\mathsf{O}\mathcal{A}\mathsf{C}\mathsf{q}\mathsf{O}\mathsf{\partial}\mathsf{L}\mathsf{b}$
wi di tsa lv wi s da si

going back $\mathcal{O}\mathsf{C}\mathsf{T}$
u tsu dv

grandmother of a group of children $\mathcal{O}\mathsf{h}\mathsf{\Gamma}\mathsf{b}$
u ni li si

Great Spirit $\mathsf{D}\mathsf{L}\mathcal{O}\mathsf{V}$
a da nv do

green corn $\mathsf{T}\mathsf{V}$ $4\mathsf{M}$
i tse se lu

33

grown person ᎤᏡᎾ
u dv na

hanging down ᎤᏁᏌᎠᎥ Ꭲ
u ne sa dv i

hay rake ᎧᏁᎦ ᎠᎩᏍᏙᏗ ᎬᎩ
ka ne s ga a gi s do di gv gi

hickory nut ᏐᎯ
so hi

hickory nut soup ᎦᎾᏥ
ga na tsi

hickory tree ᎤᎠᏁᎢ ᏠᎬᎢ
wa ne i tlu gv i

his arm, her arm ᎦᏅᎹᎢ
ga nv wa i

his neck, her neck ᎠᎩᎵᎨᏂ
a gi li ge ni

hominy place ᎦᏃᎮᏃᎢ
ga no he no i

hog sucker (fish) ᏓᏅᎨ
da lo ge

hymn book ᏗᎧᏃᎩᏍᏗ
di ka no gi s di

I know ᏥᎦᏔᎭ
tsi ga ta ha

I shout ᎨᎷᎲᎦ
ge lu hv ga

I want bread ᎦᏚ ᎠᏆᏚᎵᎭ
ga du a qua du li ha

I wish I had that ᏲᏎᎢ ᏯᎨᎢ
yo se i ya ge i

ice cream ᎦᏁᏍᏓᎳᏗᏍ ᏔᏅᎯ ᎤᏅᏗ
ga ne s da la di s ta nv hi u nv di

Indian ball sticks ᎠᏂᏯᏫᏯᎢ ᏗᎳᏍᎦᎵᏗ
a ni ya wi ya i di la s ga li di

Indian paint ᎤᏙ Ꮧ
wo di

in front ᎡᎬᏱᏠ
e gv yi tlv

It is going to rain ᏛᎦᎾᏂ
dv ga na ni

It is ready ᎤᏍᏆᎸᎮ
u s qua lv hv

It is snowing ᎫᏗᎭ
gu ti ha

large window ᎤᏔᏂᏗ ᎰᎳᏂ
u ta ni di tso la ni

Little People ᏴᏫ ᏧᎾᏍᏗᎦ
yv wi tsu na s ti ga

little spoon ᎤᏍᏗ ᏗᏙᏗ
u s di di do di

log cabin ᏧᎸᏓᎨᏫ ᎠᏁᏍᎬᏗ
tsu lv da ge wi a ne s gv di

married person ᎤᏓᏟ
u da tli

Medicine Man ᏗᏓᏅᏫᏍᎩ
di da nv wi s gi

mud turtle ᏌᎵᎫᎩ
sa li gu gi

my arm ᏥᏅᏬᎢ
tsi nv wo i

my aunt ᎠᎩᏢᎩ
a gi tla gi

my brother ᎢᎩᏅᏟ
i gi nv tli

my daughter ᎠᏇᏥ ᎠᎨᏳᏤ
a que tsi a ge yu tsa

my ear ᏥᎴᏂ
tsi le ni

my finger ᏥᏸᏌᏛᎢ
tsi ye sa dv i

my foot ᎠᏆᎳᏏᏕᏂ
a qua la si de ni

my friend ᎣᎩᎾᎵᎢ
o gi na li i

my grandfather ᎡᏚᏚ
e du du

my grandmother ᎡᎵᏏ
e li si

my hair ᎠᎩᏍᏗᏰᎬᎢ
a gi s ti ye gv i

35

my hand Ꭰ Ꮙ Ᏸ Ꮒ
a quo ye ni

my heart Ꭰ Ꮖ Ꮣ Ꮕ Ꮩ
a qua da nv do

my mother Ꭱ Ꮵ
e tsi

my son Ꭰ Ꮗ Ꮵ
a que tsi

my toe Ꮵ Ꮎ Ꮜ Ꮫ Ꭲ
tsi na sa dv i

my toes Ꮥ Ꮵ Ꮎ Ꮜ Ꮫ Ꭲ
de tsi na sa dv i

my wife Ꭰ Ꮖ Ꮣ Ꮅ Ꭲ
a qua da li i

Nantahala Ꮕ Ꮣ Ᏸ Ꮅ
nv da ye li

new-born baby Ꭴ Ꮝ Ꮧ Ꭴ Ꮣ Ꭸ Ꭲ
u s di u da ge i

New Year Ꭲ Ꮴ Ꭴ Ꮥ Ꮨ Ᏼ Ꮢ Ꭲ
i tse u de ti yv sv i

no good Ꭴ Ᏺ Ꭲ
u yo i

No, thank you Ꮭ Ꮓ
tla no

not any Ꭷ Ꮒ Ꭹ Ꮣ
ka ni gi da

Numbers Ꮧ Ꮞ Ꮝ Ꮧ
di se s di

one Ꮜ Ꮙ
sa quo

two Ꮤ Ꮅ
ta li

three Ꮶ Ꭲ
tso i

four Ꮕ Ꭹ
nv gi

five Ꭿ Ꮝ Ꭹ
hi s gi

six Ꮡ Ꮣ Ꮅ
su da li

seven ᏓᎵᏉᎩ ᏌᏟᎥᏴ
ga li quo gi

eight ᏒᎾᎳ ᏦᏞᏫ
tsu ne la

nine ᏌᏁᎳ ᏌᎾᎳ
sa ne la

ten ᎤᏍᎪᎯ ᏎᎠᎠ
s go hi

one hundred ᏎᎠᎠ ᏦᏈ
sa quo *i ya ga yv li*

one thousand ᏏᎥ ᏔᏎᏕᏟ

old field ᎤᏫᏔ ᏦᏝᎦᏏ ᏍᎦᎷ
sa quo

old field apricot drink ᎤᏣᎦ ᎠᏗᏔᏍᏗ ᎤᏣᎦ ᎠᏗᏔᏍᏗ ᎤᏬᏎᎷ

old man ᎤᎷᎦᎷᎠ

old woman ᎤᏛᏌᏅᎯ ᎠᏍᏇᏟᎥᏔ
u dv sa nv hi

One Feather ᎠᎦᏴᎵᎨᎢ ᏏᎥ ᎤᏴᎵᏟ
a ga yv li ge i

paper money ᏌᏉ ᎤᎩᏓᎵ ᎠᏎᎥ
sa quo *u gi da li*

parboil ᎠᏕᎷ ᎠᏗᏓᎠᏗ ᏕᎥᎷ ᎠᏟᏣᎷ
a de lv

Passion Flower ᎠᎬᏱ ᎠᎵᏨᏓ ᎤᎦᏎ
a gv yi *a li tsv da*

Peace on Earth ᎤᏣᎦ ᏣᎠᏕ ᎥᎠᎷ ᏥᏌᏎᏔ
u wa ga

pine cone ᎡᎶᎯᏃ ᏙᎯᏱ ᎨᏎᏍᏘ ᎤᏎᎤᏬᎠ ᏃᏦ
e lo hi no *do hi yi* *ge se s ti*

pitch fork ᎤᏍᎫᏔᏅᎯ ᏃᏥ ᏇᏴ ᏣᎢ
u s gu ta nv hi *no tsi*

place to lie down ᏴᎩ ᎡᏆ ᏫᏂᏉᏂ
yv gi *e qua*

pocket knife ᏔᏂᏏᏂ ᏦᏎᎤᏔ ᎷᎷᎷᎠ ᏇᏫ
ta ni si ni

poison ivy ᏒᏍᏈ ᏓᏗᎠᏗ ᏯᎷ ᎤᏝᎷ ᎤᎷᏓ
tsu s qui *da di a di* *ye l*
u lv da

37

poplar tree ᎢᎦᏡᎬᎢ
tsi yu tlu gv i

pottery vessel ᎥᏘ ᎠᏥᏍᏙᎢ
v ti a tsi s do i

praying mantis ᎤᏙᎳᏅᏍᏗ
u do la nv s di

rainbow trout ᏧᎶᎸᏗ ᎠᏣᏗ
tsu lo lv di a tsa di

raining afar ᏗᎦᏍᎦ
di ga s ga

red horse (fish) ᎣᎵᎦ
o li ga

rocking chair ᏍᏚᏯᎷ ᏗᎳᎷᎨᏍᎩ
ga s gi lo di la lu ge s gi

sassafras tea ᎦᎾᏍᏓᏥ ᎠᏗᏔᏍᏗ
ka na s da tsi a di ta s di

screech owl ᏩᎱᎽ
wa hu hu

Seal of Cherokee Nation ᏣᎳᎩᏱ ᎠᏰᎵ
tsa la gi yi a ye li

Seasons of the year ᏅᎩ ᎢᎦᏛᏂ
nv gi i ga dv ni

Spring ᎪᎨᏱ
go ge yi

Summer ᎪᎩ ᎠᏰᎵ
go gi a ye li

Fall ᎤᎳᎪᎰᏍᏗ
u la go ho s di

Winter ᎪᎳ
go la

Cherokee Clans ᏣᎳᎩ ᏓᏂᎳᏍᏓᏢ [1]
tsa la gi da ni la s da tly [1]

Bird Clan ᎠᏂᏥᏍᏆ
a ni tsi s qua

Paint Clan ᎠᏂᏬᏗ
a ni wo di

Deer Clan ᎠᏂᎠᏫ
a ni a wi

Panther Clan ᎠᏂᎩᎶᏗ
a ni gi lo gi

38

Wild Potato Clan ᎠᏂᎪᏓᎨᏫ
a ni go da ge wi

Blue Holly Clan ᎠᏂᏌᎰᏂ
a ni sa ho ni

Wolf Clan ᎠᏂᏩᏯ
a ni wa ya

short coat ᎦᏌᎴᎾ ᎤᏍᏆᎳᎯ
ga sa le na u s qua la hi

sick in bed ᎤᏢᎦ ᎦᏂᏏ ᎦᏅᎦ
u tlv ga ga ni si ga nv ga

sitting up ᎤᏬᏝ
u wo tla

small window ᎤᏍᏗ ᏦᎳᏂ
u s di tso la ni

someone falling off an object ᎦᎶᎣᏍᎦ
ga lo o s ga

something to cook ᎪᎱᏍᏗ ᎠᏓᏍᏓᏴᏗ
go hu s di a da s da yv di

sourwood tree ᏅᏙᏛᏯ ᏡᎬᎢ
nv do que ya tlu gv i

speckled trout (s) ᎤᏅᏣᏛ ᎠᏣᏗ
u nv tsa dv a tsa di

Speckled trout (p) ᎤᎾᏅᏣᏛ ᎠᏣᏗ
u na nv tsa dv a tsa di

spicewood tea ᏃᏓᏥ ᎠᏗᏔᏍᏗ
no da tsi a di ta s di

string of beads ᎠᏕᎳ ᏗᏯᏠᏗ
a de la di ya tlo di

striped skunk ᏧᎸᏕᏍᏗ
tsu lv de s di

sweet potato ᏄᏅ ᎤᎦᎾᏍᏛ
nu nv u ga na s dv

table fork ᏴᎩ ᎦᏍᎩᎸ ᎠᏌᏗᏍᏗ
yv gi ga s gi lv a sa di s di

table knife ᎦᏍᎸᎢ ᎠᏌᏗᏍᏗ ᏰᎳᏍᏗ
ga s lv i a sa di s di ye la s de

Tennessee ᏔᏂᏏ
ta ni si

Thank you ᏩᏙ
wa do

tiny sparrow ᏥᏍᏆᏯ
tsi s qua ya

The Removal ᏥᎨᎬᏬᎣᏔᏁᎢ
tsi ge gv wo o ta ne i

to carry ᎪᏱᏄᏍᏗ
go yi nu s di

to warm it ᎯᎦᎾᏬᏓ
hi ga na wo da

Trail of Tears ᎨᏥᎧᎲᏓ ᎠᏁᎬᎢ
ge tsi ka hv da a ne gv i

Tuckaseegee ᏓᎦᏏᏱ
da ga si yi

Tuscola ᏔᏍᎪᎳ
ta s go la

Twelve Months ᏔᎳᏚ ᎢᏯᏅᏓ
ta la du i ya nv da

January ᏚᏃᎸᏔᏂ
du no lv ta ni

February ᎧᎦᎵ
ka ga li

March ᎠᏄᏱ
a nu yi

April ᎧᏩᏂ
ka wa ni

May ᎠᎾᏍᎬᏘ
a na s gv ti

June ᏕᎭᎷᏱ
de ha lu yi

July ᎫᏰᏉᏂ
gu ye quo ni

August ᎦᎶᏂ
ga lo ni

September ᏚᎵᎢᏍᏗ
du li i s di

October ᏚᏂᏅᏗ
du ni nv di

November ᏄᏓᏕᏆ
nu da de qua

December ᎥᏍᎩᎦ
v s gi ga

ugly person	ᏂᏓᏤᎸᎾ ᏴᏫ	
	ni da tse lv na yv wi	
United States	ᎠᎹᏰᎵ	
	a ma ye li	
up the hill	ᎦᏚᏏ	
	ga du si	
very old	ᎠᎦᏴᎵ	
	a ga yv li	
walnut tree	ᏎᏗ ᏠᎫᏉ	
	se di tlu gv i	
wash day	ᏧᎾᎩᎶᏍᏗ ᎢᎦ	
	tsu na gi lo s di i ga	
water bucket	ᎠᎹ ᎠᎫᎩᏍᏗ	
	a ma a gu gi s di	
water dog	ᏧᏩ	
	tsu wa	
White man	ᎤᏁᎦ	
	yu ne ga	
White Oak Tree	Ꮤ�01 ᏠᎫᏉ	
	ta la tlu gv i	
White Pine tree	ᏲᏥ ᏠᎫᏉ	
	o tsi tlu gv i	
wild greens	ᎦᏄᎸᎯ	
	ga nu lv hi	
Angelico	ᏩᏁᎩᏛ	
	wa ne gi dv	
branch lettuce	ᎠᎹᏱ ᎤᏚᎯ ᎠᎪᏍᏓᎩᏍᏗ	
	a ma yi u du hi a go s da gi s di	
creases	ᎤᎵᏏ	
	u li si	
juwhitsgi	ᏧᎯᏧᎩ	
	tsu hi tsu gi	
phacaelia	ᎤᏕᏍᎩ	
	u s te s gi	
sochani	ᏐᏣᎾ	
	so tsa na	
sweet grass	ᎤᎦᎾᏍᏓ	
	u ga na s da	
You go first	ᎡᎬᏱ	
	e gv yi	

you go hunting TZMS
i no lu ga

young man DθΘ
a wi na

young woman DᏬ
a dv

your grandmother ᏟᏟᏏ
tsa li si

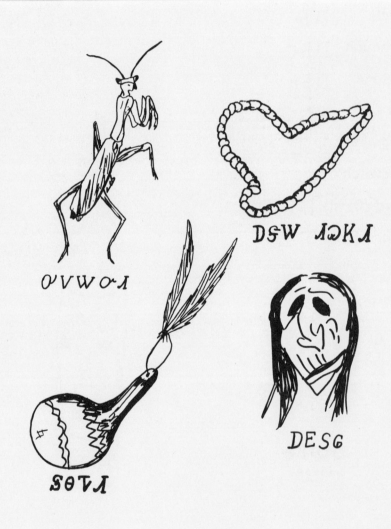

ᎧᏙᎳᏁᏗ

DᎮᏔ ᏗᏬᎧᏗ

ᏕᎧᏙᏗ

DEᏕᏉ

People - ᏴᎣ
<small>yv wi</small>

Agnes (Aggie) ᎡᏯᏂ
<small>e gi ni</small>

Alec Standing water ᎡᏟᎩ ᎠᎹᏱ ᏌᎥᏚ
<small>e li gi   a ma yi ga dv ga</small>

Amoneeta ᎠᏦᏂᏓ
<small>a mo ni da</small>

Arch ᎠᏥ
<small>a tsi</small>

Arneach ᎠᏂᏣ
<small>a ni tsa</small>

Arsene ᎠᏏᏂ
<small>a si ni</small>

Ax ᏣᎷᏩᏍᏗ
<small>ga lu wa s di</small>

Bigmeat ᎡᏆ ᎭᏫᏯ
<small>e qua   ha wi ya</small>

Bigwitch ᏍᎩᎵ ᎡᏆ
<small>s gi li   e qua</small>

Bird (Byrd) ᏥᏍᏆ
<small>tsi s qua</small>

Black Fox ᎢᏃᎵ
<small>i no li</small>

ᎤᏙᎵᎠ
cabbage

DESG
mask

Brown ᏩᏗᏰᎢ
wa di ye i

Buck ᎦᏓᎩᎾ
ga la gi na

Bushyhead ᎤᏃᏓᏘ
u no da ti

Catolster ᎦᏙᎳᏍᏓ
ga do la s da

Catt ᏪᏌ
we sa

Charley ᏣᎵ
tsa li

Chicalelee ᏣᎦᎵᎵ
tsa ga li li

Chiltoskey (or Chiltoskie) ᏥᎳᏙᎣᏍᎩ
tsi la do o s gi

Climbing Bear (or Climbing bear) ᏲᏅ ᎦᎴᎩ
yo nv ga le gi

Conseen ᎦᎾᏏᏂ
ga na si ni

Contesky ᎦᎾᏗᏍᎩ
ga na di s gi

Cornsilk ᏎᎷ ᎤᏁᏄᏗ
se lu u ne nu di

Crowe (Crow) ᎪᎬ
go gv

Cucumbe ᎦᎦᎹ
ga ga ma

Driver ᏗᏰᎴᎩ
di ye le gi

Eva ᎡᏫ
e wi

Feather ᎤᎩᏓᏟ
u gi da tli

Fox Squirrel ᏌᎶᎵᏬᏗ
sa lo li wo di

George ᏣᏥ
tsa tsi

Goingback ᎤᏨᏛ
u tsv dv

Going bird ᏢᏒᏍᎠᎣᎢ
tsi s qua a na i

Hanging Dog ᎩᏟ ᏍᏗ
gi li ga di

Hornbuckle ᎤᎰᎾ ᎠᎧᏁᏍᏗ
u yo nv a ka ne s di

Howanetta ᎠᏪ ᎠᏂᏓ
a we a ni da

John Ross ᎫᏫᏍ ᎫᏫ
gu wi s gu wi

Jumper ᏗᎳᏔᏕᎩ
di la ta de gi

Junaluska ᏧᏄᎸᎮᏍᎩ
tsu nu lv hv s gi

June ᏕᎭᎷᏱ
de ha lu yi

Kanuga ᎧᏄᎦ
ka nu ga

Kina ᎧᏱᏂ
ka yi ni

Larch ᎳᎠᏥ
la a tsi

Little-John ᎤᏍᏗ ᏣᏂ
u s di tsa ni

Locust ᎧᎶᏇᎩᏗ
ka lo que gi di

Long ᎦᏅᎯᏛ
ga nv hi dv

Lossiah ᎶᏏ
lo si

Mark ᎹᎦ
ma ga

Martha ᎹᏗ
ma di

Martin ᏧᏧ
tsu tsu

Mary ᎺᎵ
me li

Oocumma ᎤᏏᎦ
u ga ma

Oosowi ᎤᎮᎾ
u sa wi

Oostanaga ᎤᏍᏗᏁᎦ
u s di ne ga

Otter ᏥᏯ
tsi ya

Owl (Owle) ᎤᎫᎫ
u gu gu

Panther ᏔᎭᏥ
tlv da tsi

Partridge ᎫᏇ
gu que

Pheasant ᎥᏗᏍᏗ
dv di s di

Rattler ᏧᏃᏴᎩ
tsu no yv gi

Richard ᎤᏪᎾᎢ
u we na i

Running-Bear ᏲᏅ ᎠᏗᏏ
yo nv a di si

Running-Wolf ᏩᏯ ᎠᏗᏏ
wa ya a di si

Sallie ᎲᎵ
sa li

Saughee ᎲᏍᏯ
sa ga ya

Saunooke ᎲᎦᏄᎩ
s wa nu gi

Screamer ᎠᏂᏴᎳ
a ni yv la

Sequoyah ᏏᏉᏯ
si quo ya

Shell ᎤᏯᏍᎦ
u ya s ga

Shutegi ᏒᏕᎩ
su de gi

Skieg ᏍᎩᎩ
s gi gi

Skitty ᏍᎩᏗ
s gi di

Smoker ᎪᎩᏍᎩ
go gi s gi

Squirrel ᏌᎶᎵ
sa lo li

Stamper ᏗᎳᏍᎨᏍᎩ
di la s ge s gi

Standing Indian ᏴᏫᏯ ᎦᏙᎦ
yv wi ya ga do ga

Standing-deer ᎠᏫ ᎦᏙᎦ
a wi ga do ga

Swimmer ᎠᏴᎢᏂ
a yv i ni

Tahquette ᏓᏆᏗᎯ
da qua di hi

Talalah ᏓᎳᎳ
da la la

Teesateskie ᏗᏌᏕᏍᎩ
di sa de s gi

Teleski ᏓᎵᏍᎩ
da li s gi

Toineeta ᏙᏯᏂᏓ
do ya ni da

Tooni ᏙᎾᏯ
do na ya

Tramper ᏗᎳᏍᎨᏍᎩ
di la s ge s gi

Tsali ᏣᎵ
tsa li

Twister ᏗᎦᏄᏖᏲᎯ
di ga nu te yo hi

Ute ᏳᏗ
yu di

Wachacha ᏩᏣᏣ
wa tsa tsa

Waidsutte ᎤᏬᏓᏌᏘ
u wo da sa ti

Walkingstick ᎤᏙᎳᏅᏍᏗ
u do la nv s di

Washington ꮼ Ꮟ ꮥ Ꮒ
wo si da ni

Watty Ꮳ Ꮧ
wa di

Wayahneeta Ꮳ Ᏸ Ꮒ Ꮣ
wa ya ni da

West Ꮽ Ꮥ Ꮅ Ᏻ Ꭵ
wu de li gv i

Whitetree Ꭴ Ꮑ Ꭶ Ꮤ Ꮅ Ᏻ Ꭵ
u ne ga tlu gv i

Wildcat Ꭱ Ꭿ
gv he

Will Ꭼ Ꮅ
wi li

Will West Long Ꭼ Ꮅ ꮺ Ꮝ Ꮧ Ꭶ Ꮎ Ꭿ Ꮩ
wi li   we s di   ga na hi dv

Wilnota (Wilnoty) Ꭴ Ꭵ Ꮓ Ꮧ
u lv no di

Wolf (Wolfe) Ꮳ Ᏸ
wa ya

Yonaguska Ꭿ Ꮬ Ꭰ Ꭱ Ꮟ Ꭶ Ꭹ
yo nv   a gv yi s gi

Young Ꭰ Ꮜ Ꭿ
a da hi

Youngbear Ꭿ Ꮎ Ꭰ Ꮒ Ꮣ
yo nv   a ni da

Youngbird Ꮵ Ꮝ Ꮖ Ꭰ Ꮒ Ꮣ
tsi s qua   a ni da

Youngdeer Ꭰ ꮺ Ꭰ Ꮒ Ꮣ
a wi   a ni da

Youngsquirrell Ꮠ Ꮆ Ꮅ Ꭰ Ꮒ Ꮣ
sa lo li   a ni da

Arsene's Prayer
used in "Unto These Hills"

I will lift up mine eyes unto the hills, from whence cometh my help.
My help cometh from the Lord, which made heaven and earth.

Psa. 121 : 1-2.

ᏒᏒᏈ ᎤᏗᏍᏍᏏ ᎤᏋ
ᏤᎵᎷᏜᏃᏍ ᎠᏗᏎᎯᎠ–
ᎠᏜᎭᏗᏴ ᎤᏞᏫᎤᎠ
ᎠᎩᏜᏍᏎᏗᏴ ᎤᏋᏗᏴ
ᎤᏪᏃᎤᎠ ᏒᏫᎠᏗ
ᎠᏛ ᏞᎦᎠ.
ᎤᏞᏫᎤᎠ ᏗᏩᏃᎩᎠᏆ
121 : 1-2

Arsene Thompson was a Cherokee preacher who played for years the part of Elias Boudinot. He recited this prayer before the people started on the Trail of Tears.

Cherokee Songs
ᏣᎳᎩ ᏗᎧᏃᎩᏍᏗ

tsa la gi di kano gi s di

1. Sing to tune of "What a Friend We Have in Jesus"

ᏍᎢᏔᏂᏎᏍᏗ,ᏎᎭᎬ,
ᏞᏫᏗ ᏍᏔᏒᏔ;
ᎮᎬᎣᏍᏛᎬ ᎠᏴ,
ᏣᏛᎮᎩᏗ ᎮᎠ.
ᎮᎠᎯᎱ
ᎮᎠᎯᎱ
ᏍᎩᏍᎶᏍᏛᏔᎮᏗᏍᎠᏣᎠ.

2. Sing to tune of "Amazing Grace"

ᎤᏗᏪᎤᎠ ᎤᏇᎮ
ᎢᏍᏗᏆ?Ꮤ,
ᎷᎺ ᏦᏒ ᎤᎣᎦᏎ
ᎢᏍᏗᏆᎮᎤ.

When Tsali was asked if he had anything to say before facing a firing squad, he said he wanted his people to sing. They sang "Amazing Grace" as musket shots rang out.

50

Cherokee N.C.
Jan. 5th, 1947.

Mr. Stephens   Dear friend
                    I thought I would
write to you today.   I have been waiting
for you to come, as you promised to come
and see about how I have wetten Cherokee
Dictionary; Now I have writen five hundred
words, I wrot just so you can understand
very well. I put parenthesis every between
verses: others are not. I had put coma like
this: but now I puted like this "[cat's tail] [Menkeying Eeegs]
                                                        3   4
Now. If you are ready take this words
Send large envolop. ($5.00) worth and send
check or post office money order or what ever
you wish.   From
                    Will W. Long

English	Sequoyah Syllabary	Phonetic
The diseases	ᎤᎩᎫᏯᎢ	uyugi
Small Pox		unutaguwali
Chicken Pox		tsä tsŭ gä
Whoopcough		u säs gi
Measles		gä nä wo ti s gi
Mumps		ä dä yụ tso ti s gi
Influenza		u di lä gi
Compulsion		giụ wä ni gi s dyị
Headache		us ko li ädä dä hi s dä nä hi
Tooth ache		ä dä yugwä di s gi
Ear ache		ä dä li s gwä di s gi
Heart trouble		u da nụ dyụ-i u tsụ gi
Consumption		u kä yo dụ ụ dä si wä s gi
Kidney trouble		tsu dä li ä dä tsụ gi
Stomach ache		dä lō ni
Chill		u nä wä s di u dụ nä

Above is a sample page of the dictionary started by Will West Long for book publisher George Stephens in the 1940's. First comes the English word in the scholar's own handwriting, then Sequoyah's Cherokee word in characters each representing a syllable, then pronunciation in international phonetic symbols.

Mr. Long told the publisher that he had learned to write Cherokee from a boy he met at an academy south of Greensboro, N. C. This appears to have been Trinity College, later moved to Durham and later named Duke University.

Cherokee historian Dr. James Mooney did much research in the North Carolina Great Smokies. His account mentions that a bright young Cherokee boy knew the Sequoyah language and was of great help. This youth seems to have been Will West Long, who inspired this book.

CHEROKEE ALPHABET

ᏣᏔᎩ

Ꭱ_ĕ	Ꮰ_tlo	Ꮡ_kcă	Ᏺ_hnă	Ꮿ_yă
Ꭰ_ă	Ꮜ_tcă	Ꮳ_tsų	Ꮆ_lo	Ꮹ_wă
Ꮃ_lă	Ᏸ_yų	Ꮢ_sų	Ꮐ_yu	Ꮏ_tci
Ꮵ_tsi	Ꮭ_lų	Ꮒ_ni	Ꮴ_tsĕ	Ꮭ_tlă
Ꮎ_nă	Ꭿ_ci	Ꮺ_gă	Ꮧ_di	Ꮕ_mĕ
Ꮖ_wŭ	Ꮻ_s	Ꮩ_do	Ꮾ_wŭ	Ꮛ_gwų
Ꮽ_wĕ	Ꮒ_[illegible]	Ꭶ_gā	Ꮥ_dŭ	Ꮻ_gwų
Ꮭ_li	Ꮁ_ŭ	Ꮄ_dă	Ꮬ_dĕ	
Ꮑ_nā	Ꭺ_go	Ꭼ_gų	Ꮆ_tsà	
Ꮋ_mo	Ꮷ_tsu	Ꮚ_wi	Ꭵ_ų	
Ꭹ_gi	Ꮜ_mu	Ꭲ_i	Ꮑ_nų	
Ᏹ_yi	Ꮞ_sĕ	Ꮎ_u	Ꮢ_tce	
Ꮟ_si	Ꮠ_so	Ᏼ_yĕ	Ꮦ_mă	
Ꮸ_tlų	Ꮣ_tli	Ꮿ_cų	Ꮼ_sŭ	
Ꭳ_o	Ꮖ_gwi	Ꮷ_dų	Ꮲ_tlŭ	
Ꮇ_lu	Ꮕ_gwĕ	Ꭻ_gu	Ꮅ_cĭ	
Ꮄ_lĕ	Ꮷ_są	Ꮶ_tso	Ᏻ_co	
Ꮀ_că	Ꮖ_kwă	Ꮡ_gwo	Ꮋ_mi	
Ꮼ_wo	Ꮓ_no	Ꮔ_nŭ	Ꮂ_tlā	

Written by Will West Long of
Big Cove, Swain County, NC. 1947.
7/8 Cherokee, language scholar. F.M.S.

THE CHEROKEE PEOPLE

The Cherokee people have always been the mountaineers of the South. At one time they held 40,000 square miles of land now in the states of North Carolina, South Carolina, Virginia, Tennessee, Georgia and Alabama. Echota, in Tennessee, later New Echota in Georgia, were their main capital towns.

The name *Cherokee* has no meaning in the Cherokee language, but seems to have been of foreign origin. *Tsa-la-gi* is the form used at present. The language must have been related to that of the Iroquois. Mooney found three dialects of the language while he studied the background of the Cherokee in the late 1800's. The middle dialect—also known as the Kituwha—is the one spoken by the Cherokee people today.

Written records of the Cherokee date from the coming of De Soto in 1540. Farming and fishing provided their simple needs at that time. Friendships soon developed, metal working was learned from the Spanish. As other European people came into their lands, they made friends and learned from them.

By the late 1790's schools were being established, progress was moving forward quite well. But, sadly, the Cherokee people could not live apart from the happenings of the people around them. As the white people made war against each other, the Cherokee were pulled into these wars. By 1821 two great accomplishments had been gained—a written constitution patterned after the United States Constitution and an alphabet invented by Sequoyah. These should have helped the Cherokee to move along in the path of civilization as fast as his neighbors, but events worked against them.

In 1828 the United States Congress passed the Indian Removal Act which led to the tragic removal of the Cherokee to the West.

Today the Cherokee people who live on the Qualla Boundary (also called the Cherokee Indian Reservation) are the descendants of the few who hid out in the Great Smoky Mountains until they were permitted to stay there after Tsali gave his life for his people. The Cherokee today live and dress very much as do others around them. A few of them are still able to speak their beautiful language.

MARY U. CHILTOSKEY

Pictured above with the Chiltoskeys at their home in Cherokee beside the Oconaluftee River is publisher-designer George Myers Stephens.

On graduating twenty years earlier from the University of North Carolina at Chapel Hill he had gone into the Great Smokies as his timber cruiser party explored the land purchase for the national park. He wrote *The Smokies Guide* based on living in this high wilderness.

Still later he helped start the Cherokee Historical Association. It has brought alive the Cherokee-pioneer history through the outdoor drama "Unto These Hills", the Museum of the Cherokee Indian, and Oconaluftee Living Indian Village. With Samuel E. Beck, founder of the museum, he published *Cherokee Cooklore,* a book of wild food recipes compiled by Mrs. Chiltoskey.

For his career of writing, publishing, and working to reveal culture of the mountain region's people, his Chapel Hill alma mater awarded him an honorary doctoral degree.

Following success of the Cherokee Historical Association ventures to bring visitors from over the nation, Cherokee leaders with Bureau of Indian Affairs support helped in establishing the Boundary Tree Tourist Development, the Qualla Arts and Crafts Co-operative with its outstanding display, the Cherokee Community Center with its library founded by Mrs. Chiltoskey, the Trout Management Enterprise and Mingo Falls Family Campground, and foster homes for Cherokee girls and boys.

Meanwhile the tourist influx was followed by building of high class motels and eating places, scores of gift shops, splendid new churches, and even small manufacturing plants.

Early 1972 saw plans taking shape for a new Museum of the Cherokee Indian and a cluster of government-financed school buildings.

Both Goingback and Watty Chiltoskie are noted wood sculptors and model makers. Goingback has been a career carving teacher.

For more words or autographs

DATE DUE			
7			
GAYLORD			PRINTED IN U.S.A.